Bold Prayers from the Heart

Jean Maalouf

Sheed & Ward
Kansas City

Sheed & Ward™ is a service of The National Catholic Reporter Publishing Company.

Maalouf, Jean
   ISBN: 1-55612-773-1 (hardcover)
        1-55612-850-9 (paperback)

Published by: Sheed & Ward
          115 E. Armour Blvd.
          P.O. Box 419492
          Kansas City, MO 64141-6492

To order, call: (800) 333-7373

Illustrations© 1995 by Maureen Noonan. Cover design by James F. Brisson.

Contents

Introduction

MANY BOOKS OF PRAYERS HAVE BEEN WRITTEN. IT IS NOT without some hesitation that I attempt to add another book to the world's library of prayer books. This book has something special. It is neither a scholarly book, nor one that wants to prove something. It is not written in a preaching language. It is not meant to replace the prayers already known, and already said everyday with great devotion. The prayers of this book are not intended to be impersonally said in a vacuum, either. They are embedded in the heart of one's being, like a person trying to meet God in a most intimate and familiar manner. They are the prayers of one man, and they tell, in one way or another, the story of the Holy Spirit in his life. The Lord of life is best known this way—through the very act of living, in one person and in one life.

My approach is the same as the approach of Abraham and Job who had the guts to argue with God. It is a direct, intimate, straightforward, spontaneous, and bold talking with the Lord. These prayers are free speeches to God. I'll tell Him all what is going on in my mind and heart without censuring anything, be it a thought, a petition, a reflection, a feeling, a poem, a gratitude or even a rebellion. Just reflections of my daily life, and life has all these elements.

These prayers were fashioned by the man, as well as they fashioned the man. In a sense, many of them were a living story and many others made the story. That is why they are real and have nothing to do with the "parrot syndrome." A "pious and devout robot" does not make a saint. No way!

This book is neither a theology book, nor a philosophy book, nor a psychology book, nor a poetry book, in the sense of a formal treatise. It is rather a living theology and philosophy and psychology and poetry. It is the story of the Spirit in the flesh. It is a prayerful life-style. This is what counts most. If I were to give a title to my method, I should call it something like "incarnational spirituality," "secular holiness," "existential spirituality," "human experience of God," or maybe a "deification in progress" . . . Saint Athanasius who said of Christ, "He was made man that we might be God"; Saint Basil the Great, for whom man is nothing less than a creature that has received the order to become God; and Saint Maximus the Confessor, and other early Fathers, and even the Fathers and Mothers of the Desert would have applauded this appellation. They didn't think either, that spirituality should be an abstraction. They rather talked about the way the souls of human beings work, and what we need to know and practice in order to become what we are meant to be. Saint Paul and Saint John were even more radical. In many, many places in their letters, they mentioned the necessity to see the Lord in the here and now, for "in Him who is the source of my strength I have strength for everything" (Philippians 4:13). And in our modern times, writers like the monk Thomas Merton, the Jesuit Teilhard de Chardin, Mother Theresa of Calcutta, and many others have made it clear that contemplative spirituality was not what the hermits do all day and night long, and it was not a purely monastic concern. *Spirituality has become everyone's concern.* Books about meditation and prayers are written by the thousands all over the world, and millions of people find great interest in them.

So, gone are the days in which holiness—as was the widespread assumption in spirituality—was the specialty of the priest, the hermit, the monk, the nun or any person in the hierarchical clergy. *Everyone is called to holiness* anytime, anywhere, with any "real" issue or concern we face: war and peace, poverty, relationship, sorrow, joy, pursuit of power and influence, and so forth, for the world that God "had made and He found it very good" (Genesis 1:31), is the real shrine of life. And even the market can be a way to God, as asceticism is. Still we should go to church, participate in the Eucharist, and in any religious activity. But our religious life is not meant to stop there. Rather, there it may begin with the sacraments and the word of God. When we make all of our life sacramental and prayerful, the church, then, and the words we hear in the church, as well as the sacraments we participate in, will make more sense.

How many minutes do we spend with God in a week time period? Sixty minutes on Sunday, ten minutes in the morning, ten minutes in the evening, on any other day of the week. This makes about three hours out of a total of one hundred sixty eight hours. What a difference! Three hours for God and one hundred sixty five hours for sleeping, eating, working and whatever we decide to do. But why not make all these hours a prayer too? This is what Paul, especially, wants us to do when he writes: "The fact is that whether you eat or drink—whatever you do—you should do all for the glory of God" (1 Corinthians 10:31), and this is what this book is all about. Continuous prayer. A prayer in action. A "deification in progress." A declaration of "the right to holiness." A "secular sainthood." A transformation of the ordinary into spiritual reality.

I have not presented these prayers in a logical manner. Prayers for this circumstance and prayer for that circumstance are not ordered. Rather, I have chosen to keep them spontaneous and wild as they came, like life itself. And this is how the Lord probably likes us to be. He looks deeply into our hearts and does not care much about logic and formality. He accepts us with our ordinary ways—exactly as we are.

I am confident that the illustrations by Maureen Noonan will help to create a powerful prayerful climate. Blank spaces here and there invite the reader to chart his or her own spiritual journey. The reader may want to add something to a particular prayer or reflect on that line or say something to the Lord from his or her own experience. This is the place to do it. Who said that a book should remain clean. What is the use of a clean book sparkling on the shelf? Don't be afraid to write on this book!! Use the book to agree; to disagree. Add to it. Cross over it. Strike out these or those words. Underline words you like. I will be the happiest person in the world if these prayers become even disfigured on the paper if they would have inspired you to become closer to the Lord. Then they would have helped you to start to enjoy the pleasure of His company wherever you are and in whatever you do!!

This book was not written in one single period of time, and there are many people who helped me write it. I am eternally grateful to the saints, mystics, masters, pioneers, visionaries, explorers, seekers, adventurers who dared to live, pray, and believe in the inherent goodness of the ordinary living and all life. I was inspired greatly by the Psalms of David and by the writings of Saint John, Saint Paul, Saint Benedict, Saint Augustine, Saint John Chrysostom, Saint Basil, Saint Anselm, Saint Thomas Aquinas, Saint Irenaeus, Saint Ephraim, Saint Maximos the Confessor, Saint Francis of Assisi, Saint John of the Cross, Saint Patrick, Meister Eckhart, Thomas a Kempis, Julian of Norwich, Martin Luther. And in a more recent time, I was also inspired by the writings of Saint Theresa of Lisieux, Pope John XXIII, Soren Kierkegaard, Teilhard de Chardin, Dietrich Bonhoeffer, Christina Rossetti, Dag Hammarskjold, Mother Teresa of Calcutta, Robert Schuller, M. Williamson, Horton Davies, J. Barrie Shepherd, Malcolm Boyd, Eizabeth Goudge, Thomas Merton, Henri Nouwen, William Johnson, William McNamara, Louis Evely, Michel Quoist, Bede Griffiths, and many others. I acknowledge everyone of them as I acknowledge everyone of my parents, relatives, teachers and friends. All of them were directly or indirectly involved in this book. And in a more direct way, I acknowledge the invaluable help of Joan Foster who has kindly read through the book, given precision to the language, and made pertinent suggestions emerging from her intuitive heart, spiritual depth and religious insights. Also, I would like to give a particularly deep bow to Robert Heyer, Editor-in-Chief of Sheed & Ward and his staff for their understanding, encouragement, support and assistance for the accomplishment and success of this project.

I dedicate this book to the Friend who was with me when I wrote these lines, who is and will be here, now and always, and whom I meet everyday, when I meet every person. Thank You, Lord, for Your presence that makes all the difference in the world. Now I know that WITH YOU, "I have strength for everything." Now I know how much I need You in a bold journey like this. Blessed are they who have the essential connection.

On the Incarnation Day

Lord,

What shall I offer You on this day of Your Incarnation?
I have neither gold, nor silver, neither myrrh, nor incense.
I have no settled home.
I have no space for You.
I have no room for You.
My soul is confused, my heart divided, my mind undecided.
My eyes are too blind, to look beyond the circle of myself.
My ears are too deaf, to listen to other than whatever my whims demand.
My hands are empty.
My feet do not fit into the right steps.
My voice is not clear, to sing You a love song.
My lips are not clean, to cover you with tender kisses.
For a long-time, I was like Peter who denied You, and like Judas who doubted and sold You.

And You have kept knocking at my door, for years and years.

I have never invited You in, for I do not wear the right garment, and my table is congested with the things You do not like.

I have no room for You.

But
You managed to come into a crib.
Your manger was a disclosure to my artificial excuses, and an uprootal of my deficient categories and structures and infrastructures.
Your extreme simplicity was a slap in the face to my many superfluous things and a destruction to my varied idols.
Your light set on fire all my old values, images, concepts, logic, philosophy and way of life that I used to cherish and revere.
Your infinite love was the answer to my incessant conflicts with myself, and with others. Your love was the way, the

only way, for wedding and blending heaven and earth, and for unity and peace.

Lord,

What can I offer You on this day of Your Incarnation?

I have nothing to offer You but myself.

I offer You my confused soul, my divided heart, and my undecided mind.

I offer You my eyes, my hands, my feet, my whims, my anxieties, my worries, my mistakes, my dissatisfactions, my ingratitude, my depression, my boredom, my resentment, my reluctance, my contradictions, my compromises, and my vulnerability.

I offer You my deceiving certitudes, my disingenuous interpretations, my phony criteria, my adaptive knowledge, my "religious" prejudices, my improper laws, my two-faced calculations, my poor relativity, my everlasting hesitations, my so-called truths, and my perpetual fluctuations.

I offer You my longing to be useful, effective, successful, performing, producing, excelling, and competing.

I offer You my brothers and sisters who are without shelter, without bread, without water, without home, without security, and without liberty.

I offer you my indifferences too, Lord.

Please Lord,

It is You who can make all things new.

Plunge me into the ocean of Your love. Your love will become the very ground of my being.

Give me the only water which quenches my thirst.

Give me Your eyes, Your ears, Your heart. I want to see only what You see. I want to hear only what You hear. I want to love only what You love.

Give me Your simplicity. I have to get rid of these many things which encumber my life.

Give me Your light. Too many people, like me, are still unaware of Your real You. Too many people, like me, are still overwhelmed by masks and unreal appearances.

Lord,

What shall I offer You on this day of your Incarnation?

My only gift to You is myself.

Please, Lord, don't reject it for its falsehood, and its distortion.

I offer You myself and wait for Your Words.

Only Your words make all things new, and can make me according to You.

Happy Birthday!

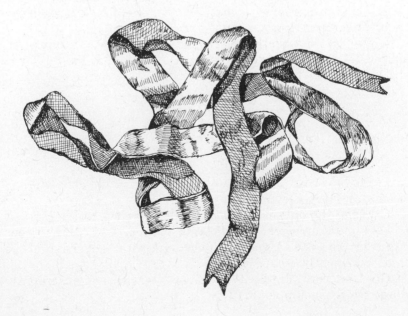

Forgive Me, Lord

Forgive me, Lord, for having forgotten that You were the Infinite Love that came down among us, and for not letting myself be loved as you wanted me to be loved.

Forgive me, Lord, for having made Your trip on earth almost useless. I refused to receive You neither in my home, nor in my soul.

Forgive me, Lord, for having preferred to send You back to where You came from, as if I wasn't in need of You.

Forgive me, Lord, for having used You as a tranquilizer for my restless mind and my tormented heart, as if You were the magical drug for any crisis.

Forgive me, Lord, for having taken You as a mere topic for discussion, as if You were a mathematical equation to be proved or to prove something.

Forgive me, Lord, for having deformed Your face, as if You were the object of my whims and fantasies.

Forgive me, Lord, for having mutilated You and reducing You to a ridiculous caricature many, many times.

Forgive me, Lord, for having used You as an effective weapon against those who do not believe in You, as if salvation was a political campaign rather than a grace coming from You and the work of the Holy Spirit.

Forgive me, Lord, for having taken You as a Commander-in-Chief for a large army of believers, those who follow strictly Your orders in order to get to eternal life, as if eternal life was something different from You who are "the way, and the truth, and the life" (John 14:6), and the "eternal life" (1 John 5:20).

Forgive me, Lord, for having solicited favors from You through prayers, fasts, sacrifices, as if You were the wealthy and powerful Being, who generously dispenses these things from far, far away.

Forgive me, Lord, for having not let You be involved in my personal life and daily activities, as if You were not the ground of my very being and the source of my very activities.

Forgive me, Lord, for not having been able to let others detect You in me.

Forgive me, Lord, for having crucified You again, as if one time was not enough.

Forgive me, Lord, and help me to see You again as You really are.

Praise to You, Lord

Praise to You, Lord,

> For the boundless sky, the sparkling stars, and the
> vast oceans.
> For the fresh air, the brilliant light, and the
> deepest darkness.
> For days, nights, and seasons.
> For the mountains, rivers, and seas.
> For the flowing oil, the powerful atom, and the
> hovering satellites over our planet.
> For science, technology, and electronics.
> For Scriptures, spirituality, and poetry.
> For artists, technicians, and scholars.
> For all men, women and children.
> For everyone and everything.

Praise to You, Lord,

> For the matter You have created and all the workers
> on earth who know how to take this matter and
> use it, transform it and make it a meeting place
> of Your divine action and their human activity.

Praise to You, Lord,

> For showing us Your eternal plan of LOVE that pulls
> the great movement of the universe forward, and
> everything in it, towards You.

Praise to You, Lord,

> For leading our eyes to see You everywhere in this
> limitless universe, and in every step of its
> evolution in Your direction.

Praise to You, Lord, praise to You!!

Newness

Lord,

Isn't that strange to see how things change so quickly in this world?!

Nothing remains the same. Not one single thing, Lord. Nothing.

Is mobility Your way, and flexibility Your life-style?

Is it in the absence of security, we find Your desire,

and in the absence of certainty, Your wish?

Is dissatisfaction an invitation to Your infinite attraction and disappointment a cry out to Your endless joy?

Is newness a closeness to Your might and evolution a deepening intimacy with Your light?

Dear Lord,

Is the continuous change, Your path, and the will of the Father, Your only unmoving determination? And that is why, on the one hand, You did not have a place to lay Your head, and, on the other hand, You wanted to make sure that whatever You were doing was always according to the will of the One who sent You?

Please Lord, grant me that open-hearted attitude and trust You had, and let Your Spirit lead my life, me too, where He pleases to take me. Amen.

I Love You

Lord,

    I love you so much. Amen.

Light

Dear Lord,

    Without Your light,

        My search is in vain,
        My studies and inquiries are fruitless,
        My work is useless,
        My production is senseless,
        My wealth is worthless.

Dear Lord,

        Let me not linger anymore in ignorance, skepticism
           and doubt.
        Be the Center of my centers.
        Fill all my being with You.
        Be my light, so I can see.
        Then, every thing will start to make sense.
        Then whatever I do will be worthwhile.

On the New Year's First Day

Dear Lord,

This day is the first day of a new year.

I felt this day in a special way, this year, because it was only with You.

The only time I got out was to go to the church and to express my gratitude to You and say:

Thank You, Lord, for the past year.

Thank You for the day, the night, the space, and the time.

Thank You for the health, the job, and the opportunities.

Thank You for the friends, known and still unknown.

And thank You especially for You ARE and YOU are with me.

But let me feel Your presence more openly in this coming year.

Let me feel Your peace more deeply in my family, my friends, in the world, and mainly in myself.

Let me feel Your caring hands more concerningly in everyone and in every little thing.

Let me feel Your loving heart more intimately in every heart I meet.

Let me feel Your growth more intensely in every good will.

Let me feel more unity in my Church community, in this earth and in the entire universe.

Let my eyes detect You in everyone, in every event, and in everything.

Let me be vulnerable enough to You, more transparent, so that others can see You more clearly in my life.

Let me be closer to You in whatever I do.

Lord, let this year be a holy year!

Thank You, Lord. Amen.

Thanksgiving of a Simple Worker

Thank You, Lord, for what You have given me! To be with friends, have a job, a house, space, and time, and especially a good family.

Thank You, Lord, for having allowed me to work, and to create things with You.

Thank You, Lord, for having kept me safe in a hazardous place, and on risky roads.

Thank You for my eyes, so I can see what I am doing, and why.

Thank You for my ears, so I can hear what is good, and what is wrong.

Thank You for my hands, for they are always handy, and for my fingers, for I can put things together with precision.

Thank You for my feet, for I can walk to take care of my machine, and for what it makes, and I can run to correct mistakes, and find misplaced things.

Thank You for my co-workers, who are also my friends, most of the time. If they happen not to be so, thank you for helping me to convince myself that my point of view is not necessarily the most suitable one.

Thank You for my bosses, for they are open and understanding. If they happen to be otherwise, thank you for helping me to imagine myself for a few seconds at the responsible post they have.

Thank You for allowing me to transform energy into production, the production into profits, the profits on progress, the progress on excellence, the excellence into loving hands and caring.

And,

Forgive me, Lord, for I used to take all these things for granted. I used to forget that they are Your continuous gifts to me. Please, Lord, don't let me lose my gifts at anytime.

"Cast Your Net Off the Starboard Side"

Dear Lord,

I have trouble dealing with some people, You know that, don't You?

Sometimes, people are unbearable, and in some other instances, I am the unbearable one.

I have trouble dealing with myself, You know that, don't You?

Sometimes, my split personality is unendurable too; what I want to do is so far from what I am. The worst is that I very often do not even know what I want to do.

My body's needs push me in one direction. My soul's aspirations are in another.

My heart is sometimes divided, my mind confused and my self false.

I, for a long-time, wanted to get out of this awful situation. But old habits in me die hard.

Please, Lord, put in my way the messenger who can really help me. Not by words, but by actions, by attitudes, by availability, by understanding, and by loving me.

I went around knowing Your creatures seeking an unknown, a solution, something or someone different. I worked in this quest for nothing.

I still have empty hands, empty mind, empty heart.

Yet, my faith is firm! YOU.

Let me hear where to cast my net, Lord. Speak to me.

You told the disciples: "Cast your net off to the starboard side" (John 21:6).

Please, Lord, do it again, just for me.

"Come to Me"

Dear Lord,

I am sure I wouldn't want to do it, except that you asked me.

Today, I feel terribly lonely, depressed, vulnerable and rejected from my family, from the people I work with, from everybody else too, my friends included. Nobody seems to understand. I just feel ready to put a sign over my head saying "Danger 24 hours a day. Keep away."

Yet, You asked me to love them all.

How, Lord, can I do that? Isn't that crazy!

How can You ask me such an impossible thing? It does not look right. It's not logical.

Honestly, I cannot figure You out today, dear Lord.

Wouldn't You leave me alone today, Lord? I cannot stand anybody today. Any other human voice seems a sword cutting into my aching entire body and heart and soul. Then add to this the terrible fear that is invading my whole being. There is a fear of living life the wrong way, the fear of making wrong choices, the fear of not having something to look for, the fear of condemnation, and the fear of FEAR.

Lord, it is getting dark around here, too dark. I am threatened by my own confusion. I feel destroyed. I hate myself.

I wish to sleep, sleep, sleep and not think about anything anymore, just as if nothing has ever existed.

I just want my brain to stop. I want to disappear. Perhaps then, I will be happy.

I do not want Your heaven and I do not believe in Your hell. I know nothing of heaven, I am already in hell.

BUT,

I, somehow, still hear what one time You said: "Come to me, all you who are weary and find life burdensome, and I will refresh you" (Matthew 11:28).

Lord, this is what I am going to do, and nothing else. Is that clear?

So, take all my burdens and troubles and worries and frustrations and depression and do something with them. I need to be "refreshed." Please, Lord, do something, and refresh me.

Up Again

Oh, Lord! What a beautiful day this is today!

I am up again.

Yesterday, I was mean, mean, mean with everybody, with myself and even with You. I do not know how anybody can put up with me.

I had the blues yesterday. I saw everything red.

Today, I feel much better, I see things bright, colored and green.

Those people I hated yesterday were not that bad after all. They are not perfect, but they are good people. We may disagree, but they do not really hate me. They are just as human as I am. Very often we do not know what we are doing.

Now I want to go out again and share my joy and laughter! I want to give a little child a toy or a yellow pencil. I want to light a candle in some lonely heart. Maybe, by doing so, Lord, the world will be a little brighter. Then I will feel much better too.

Honestly, my mood would never have shifted, if You did not intervene, dear Lord.

Thank You, Lord! You have cooled me down, You have taken hold of me. Thank You, Lord, thank You.

No Résumé Required

Thank You, dear Lord, for accepting me and loving me as I am now, at this very moment, unconditionally.

I do have a certain personality, a certain character and a certain vision. But also, I do have a lot of shortcomings, weaknesses, laziness, or just a certain lousy pattern for doing things.

Lord, You never asked about my qualifications. You were interested in my heart, not in my resume, indeed.

Thank You, Lord, for not asking me about my past. With You, I always feel fresh and new. Please accept me with my work-a-day clothes, my soiled hands, my split being and my unlisted sins. Let me realize that Your divine light is never clear enough, because it has always to pass through the prism of my human temperament, colored by my limitations, way of thinking, prejudices and narrow range of seeing.

But, even though, I want to know the fullness of You and live by the inflowing of the Holy Spirit. How much I wish to be able to say: "The life I live now is not my own; Christ is living in me" (Galatians 2:20). I need to say it now, dear Lord, not next week or the week after, but now.

I know that there are numerous obstacles that stand in my way, such as my temperament, my love for pleasure, my sick indecisions, my many divisions and "civil war" within me.

But, dear Lord, do not despair of me. Just help me to understand these obstacles and turn them to a starting point to go forward.

Help me to go forward.

Somehow, I am a little consoled when I read what Your apostle Paul had to say one day: ". . . I was given a thorn in the flesh, an angel of Satan to beat me and keep me from getting proud. Three times I begged the Lord that this might leave me. He said to me, 'My grace is enough for you, for in weakness power reaches perfection.' And so I willingly boast of my weakness instead, that the power of Christ may rest upon me. Therefore I am content with weakness, with mistreatment, with distress, with persecutions and difficulties for the sake of Christ; for when I am powerless, it is then that I am strong" (2 Corinthians 12:7-10).

Please, Lord, let Your Holy Spirit work in the depths of my being. I need to be healed right there.

Simplicity

Lord,

I've probably learned Your lesson. You put me in the simple atmosphere of workers, to learn to be simple too.

Thirty years You lived hidden, simple, unknown, and "unseen."

You were not an important personality in Your society.

You did not seek fame. You did not seek money. You did not seek public office. You were not a doctor in anything. and yet, You are our way of life.

The doctors, Luke said, wanted to learn from You.

Simplicity is your way.

Be my way, dear Lord.

The Right Address

Dear Lord,

Forgive my ignorance, forgive the ignorance of those who taught me that You were far away, where You are not. Always there and never here.

I thought You were in the churches, the convents and the sacristies.

I thought You were hidden somewhere in the millions of books written about You, in some unfamiliar theology, or in some intricate philosophical system.

I thought You were somewhere beyond the stars, the moon and wherever my telescope cannot reach.

I forgot, Lord, that You loved the world so much that You became flesh among us, one of us, so that the secular worldly life of ours could become your chosen residence.

I forgot—maybe I even thought it was not possible—that Your address was in our everyday life, with me.

I forgot—maybe I even did not want You to be involved in what I was doing—that You were in the mundane realm of running a machine, driving a car, baking breads, cooking eggplants, making carrot juice, emptying my garbage basket, playing tennis, writing a book, and sweating in this hot weather.

I forgot—maybe I did not even want to believe—that You like to be right in the factories, shops, offices, farms, in the political parties and government agencies, in the relationships between nations, ethnic groups and social classes and divisions, in the thousands of different faiths and in the millions of various beliefs and opinions that claim You and claim the truth, in the countless homes, rich and poor, in the press, radio and television, in the next door neighbor, and in every man and woman I meet, or I may never have the chance to meet.

I forgot—maybe I did not want to admit—that You wanted to live on every street, be in the small apartment that has no heat and no air conditioning, in my ever demanding partner, and my annoying children.

Please Lord, forgive me for forgetting Your correct address. Forgive me for having looked for You where You were not, so far away, while You promised to be with us, one of us, in us, right here until the end of time.

Please Lord, be totally involved with me and forget my forgetfulness.

Creativity

Dear Lord,

This machine I am working on is becoming very sophisticated. It is just marvelous.

But more marvelous is the intelligence which made it.

Thank You, Lord, for putting within us, our intelligence.

Thank You for allowing us to continue the work on earth which You have started.

Thank You for giving us, Lord, the power of creativity.

I Turned My Finger Towards You

"Zero defect! Outstanding!," they told me yesterday at work.

Ten years with perfect attendance, no accidents, no laziness.

A fellow worker shook hands with me, but I immediately turned my finger towards You, Lord.

I am most grateful to You, dear Lord.

Any good I have, is Your gift to me.

Any bad thing I have, it's only my own invention.

Lord, don't be hard on me. I am trying my best to improve in any area of my life. I count on You. Without You, I am obviously the weakest.

Don't let bad happenings overwhelm me. I am sure that, with You, nothing can beat me.

Don't let anything occur, that together we cannot handle.

Together, we can always do an "outstanding" job. Together we can have "zero defect" at work and elsewhere.

Thank You, Lord.

You are the one, who takes care of all His children. Make me a more grateful and an ever progressing son in the ways of your Kingdom.

Businesses

Lord,

Today I thought about the various businesses in the city.

I thought about all these men and women who come to work every single day, and exchange their services for some money, money that allows them to pay all their many bills, and survive with their families.

I thought about the great confidence You put in these men and women who have been selected to continue the work of Your creation.

I thought about the mysterious bonds that gather people together to run a particular business, through the special talents You gave them, and all the motivations that exist behind the decisions to choose to work together.

Dear Lord, make all their work holy. Let the vendor pay attention to the person who is buying, more than what this person is buying. And let the buyer pay attention to the vendor more than to the receipt for what was bought.

Dear Lord, be my companion today in that shopping center.

Grant goodness with strength, openness with courage, patience with efficiency during these long hours of work, to all the businesspersons of the city.

Lord, give us all our daily bread.

Forgive us, Lord, if we are too tempted by the demon of exploitation, unreasonable profits and artificial paradises.

Let our eyes always see You, dear Lord, in our businesses, as we try to see You in our churches.

"Religious"

Lord, today I am annoyed, upset, disgusted and probably revolted too.

My neighbors keep saying they are "religious," because they know what the Bible says, and where the Church stands in every issue. They observe apparently all moral laws, they perform all the rituals and ceremonies that are required for a religious service. Also they put money, even generously, into the Sunday collection basket.

Good for them.

But all these practices, important though they are, never convinced me, that they make anyone religious.

You are not something, dear Lord, you are SOMEONE.

You are not a God-object, neither a God-idea, nor a God-morality, nor a God of social order and discipline, nor a God of "charities." You are a God-person of love.

So, it is how I connect with others and how available I am to them and vulnerable and communicative and loving, that makes me religious, not just to perform "religious acts."

To love my neighbor, as I love You, is what religion is basically all about.

A Church is a communion in the first place, a community of love.

There was no communion in our community today. Lord, this is what bothers most today.

Please Lord, help us to keep You in our religious community as the heart and soul of our union and communion.

A Thank You Card

Lord,

I thank You:

for everything You've given me,
for my family, my friends, my country, my freedom,
for my talents and the physical, intellectual and
spiritual gifts You've granted me,
for my education, and the many books I am able to
read,
for my general health, my eyes, my hands and my feet,
for the many opportunities You put on my way,
for the possibility to grow Your way,
for opening my eyes to detect You in the events and
circumstances that encompass my life, and in my
brother and sister where You also dwell,
and for allowing me, through my job, to make a
contribution to the wonderful work You have
started in the act of creation.

Thank You, Lord, thank You for everything You've given
me.

Strange

Dear Lord,

I am dying to tell You something, right now, in front of this machine.

Here, in this noisy atmosphere and among these simple workers, I do not have even a piece of paper. Would you mind if I write on a piece of cardboard from our raw material?

Do You know what?

It is not always easy to follow your teachings here.

World values are completely different. They are upside down, and very often, they are opposite to yours.

Contradictions, so many contradictions exist here.

Politics, there is so much politics too.

Your name is forgotten, except in some rare cases.

I found myself very special, strange, eccentric and bizarre, with Your teachings in the world.

I thought I should be like that. Am I wrong?

Please, Lord, tell me and keep me Your ways.

"Give Me a Drink"

Dear Lord,

Please allow me to sit at the side of that well, as you did 2000 years ago. Allow me to ask a passer-by for a drink.

Oh! How many people are waiting for such a request. How many people need to be needed, I know, at this moment in time.

The paralyzed, the frustrated, the distressed, the indifferent, the self-centered, the discouraged, the disgusted, the hundred-time disappointed, the deformed, the weaklings, the dwarfs, the rejected, the lonely, the depressed, the heart-broken, the intimidated, the defeated, and those who are in despair and no longer know how to grow or try to grow or want to grow.

Please, Lord, let me not pass by all these wounded people without seeing them.

Maybe they need my help and maybe they do not need my help. But they surely need to be needed.

I am going to ask them for help.

Thank You, Lord, for teaching me to ask for a drink.

Did You really need the drink, Lord, when You were the very source of all life?

"Give me a drink."

My pride is shattered. The wounded are reinvigorated. The world is reactivated. My world is centered again on You.

Lord, help me to pay attention to my brother and sister at the proper time, the proper place, in the proper way.

And help me to ask them to give me something, to give something for others and to give again and again, until they are able to give of themselves. Then Lord, we'll be truly brothers and sisters in You.

I Wish You Had Died

Dear Lord,

Why are Your lessons the cause of terrible conflicts and fratricidal wars?

Why in Your name, do people kill people?

Why are these wars called "Holy wars"? Do You really want someone to murder someone else to please You? Are You really delighted to see this kind of warfare?

Dear Lord, some philosophers said that You've died. I wish it was true.

I wish You've died, long before, in the mind and words of those who believe that You are their beliefs and dogma and ideas and moralities and politics.

I wish you've died in all those merchants who took advantage of You and conducted big business on Your name.

I wish You've died long before You became beautiful words and famous speeches. Words and speeches give rise to religions and churches which preach comforting certainties, while they simply are rival sovereign fragments.

I wish You had died.

I wish You will rise again the way You really are.

Silence

Dear Lord,

You love silence.

You are silence.

Silence unites us, while words divide us. Silence gathers us together, while words scatter us. Silence invites us to peace, while words stir us to wars.

You are silence, simple silence, eloquent silence, active silence, contemplative silence.

Didn't You spend thirty years out of thirty-three in silence, dear Lord? Didn't You spend forty days in silence before You started Your public life? And how many times You retired to a mountain to spend some time alone in silence? Aren't You here, right now, in the Eucharist, in perfect silence?

Lord, teach me to be simple and silent. I will be simple and silent when I learn to look beyond appearances. Convince me that my thoughts are not Your thoughts. I must be silent to be able to listen to what You are saying. Then my words will all make sense.

For a messenger of God, silence is not the goal of his words. Quite the opposite. His words must be the vehicle of silence. For God does not speak in words. His only language is grace. His Spirit meets with our spirit in the loving silence not with words, but with a warm embrace.

Lord, teach me to be simple as a flower, silent as the silent night in the mountain and courageous to transmit your message through the silent words that give life not death.

Help me, dear Lord, to say less and to be more. Words can be wars. Silence is peace. Words are passive, silence is active. Words are complicated, silence is simple. Religion is complicated, You are simply, love.

Help me to be eloquently silent—exactly as You are.

Pray for Me

Lord,

    I am in trouble.

    Please Lord, pray for me. Amen.

I Cannot Sleep

Oh! Lord! Dear Lord!

I am just exhausted, so exhausted that I cannot even sleep.

I am dying for a good night of rest. I convinced myself that I should cool down, be quiet and I should not worry. I even took sleeping pills, and nothing worked.

I tried to lay down on one side, then on the other side, then on my stomach, then on my back, then I rotated again and again. I couldn't sleep, Lord. Nothing worked.

Please Lord, wouldn't You help me to sleep?

Then wake me up in the morning to Your mysterious ways and stay with me all day long, and I am sure that next night will take care of itself.

"Dependent"

Dear Lord,

I've always had this feeling of coming from "upstairs"!

I've had the feeling of the one who "has" and who takes care of the have-nots,

The feeling of the one who "knows" and who gives instructions to those who know not,

The feeling of the one who "gives" and who is "needed." never the one who "needs" someone else.

How satisfying it is to be needed by others!

How humiliating it is to be in need of others!

What a gift of pride! Is it a gift?

Please, Lord,

    Help me to "give" less and ask for more.
    Help me to give up this attitude of "benefactor"
        by learning to need others.
    Help me to abandon this father figure, and to be
        a real brother to my brothers and sisters.
    Help me to come down from "upstairs," and be
        "dependent" of anyone else.

Act of Giving

Lord,

Help me to be true and honest with myself in the first place.

If I give money to those who are in need, let me not be satisfied with that act of charity, if I do not offer them, at the same time, my thoughts, my hands and my heart. Let me not give out of abundance, but out of a deep sensitivity and a caring concern.

If I give and then realize that, in some way, I was the one who was given too, would this be an act of giving?

If I give with the hope that things would come back to me doubled, would this be an act of giving?

If I give with the expectation of being praised or of attracting more respect from others, would this be an act of giving?

If I give with the hidden feeling that I am rich in pride and vanity and arrogance and self-esteem, would this be an act of giving?

Lord,

Teach me to share what I have without feeling that I am the recipient, until it even hurts.

Lord,

Help me to be true and honest with myself in the first place.

Make My Day Holy

Lord,

    Today, make my day holy. Amen.

Friends

Lord,

There are people who mean so much to us—those who accept us as we are in any situation, and those to whom we can go at any time.

Thank You, Lord, for these understanding friends.

There are people who mean so much to us—those with whom we can talk and to whom we can open our hearts and minds and say exactly what is there without fear or apprehension. We know that they will support us in carrying out our dreams and in managing our failures.

Thank You, Lord, for these trustful friends.

There are people who mean so much to us—those whose wisdom held us back from mistakes, we could have made.

Thank You, Lord, for these wise friends.

There are people who mean so much to us—those in whose presence we feel energetic, straightforward and ready to meet any challenge.

Thank You, Lord, for these inspiring friends.

There are people who mean so much to us—those whose lives embody your words and whose actions point always in Your direction, those in whom we've encountered You!

Thank you, Lord, for these glorious friends of Yours, and of mine too.

"Remember Me"

Dear Lord,

Do "Remember me."

I hope it will work for me too, as it did one time for even a criminal, when You were there on the cross.

Lord, do "Remember me."

Then I Will Be Free

Dear Lord, you said: "If the Son frees you, you will really be free" (John 8:36).

Well, I do not feel free.

At least, not yet.

I am captive to myself.

I am captive to my heavy baggage—physical, mental and emotional,

I am captive to my multiple worries and superficial preoccupations,

I am captive to my knowledge and my relationships,

I am captive to my plans for the future, and for the direction I should take in my life and why and how to get there,

I am captive to my dreams, opinions and false conceptions,

I am captive to my concerns: what to read, what to write and what to say,

I am captive to the past events in my life, past patterns and past ideas,

I am captive to what I was indoctrinated, programmed and what I thought it was true,

I am captive to my body, sensations and feelings,

I am captive to all what is not me—although I cannot deny that they are part of me,

I am captive to my own ways, my own will and my own interests.

Oh! Dear Lord!

Today, more than ever before, I feel like a slave bound in all kinds of chains that blind my eyes and prevent me from seeing You in my life.

Although I wanted You to be part of my life, I managed somehow to keep You away, outside my realities.

I was afraid of You. I was afraid that You will free me. I am so attached to my attachments.

How can I keep living such a hypocrisy?!
Come over here, dear Lord, right where I do not want You to come.
Let me stop playing this game of double life.
Be involved totally in my life.
Then I will live totally.
Then I will be my real self.
Then I will be free.

Break

Lord,

Do You mind if I ask You for a break, today?

But please keep me in Your mind, and keep Your hand on my shoulder. Amen.

Beauty

Lord,

Thank You for beauty wherever it might be.

In the immense heavens, or on the fruitful earth.
In the vast oceans, or in the wide waving plains.
In the tallest tree, or in the tiniest violet.
In the flight of an eagle, or in the strength of a lion.
In the dreaming moon of a clear summer night, or in a falling rain of a severe winter day.
In the arching sky, or in the blowing winds.
In the driving clouds, or in the constellations on high.
In the human face, or in the sound of music.
In the act of compassion and hospitality, or in the attitude of openness, acceptance and forgiveness.
In a rewarding friendship, or in an everlasting love.

Thank You, Lord, for all beauty, wherever it is.

Thank You for our senses by which we can see the splendor of the morning, hear the joyous song of love, smell the fragrance of the springtime, touch and taste and feel Your Divine Presence everywhere.

To beauty, I bow my head and my heart gratefully and in reverence, for beauty is part of the Ultimate BEAUTY that YOU ARE.

Why?

Dear Lord,

When love is so abundant, so generous and so available—why do some people hate?

When knowledge is such a power, and so accessible—why allow ignorance to have great power of death?

When peace is the hope in everyone's mind, heart, will and lips—why is violence still everything?

When creativity is exciting and rewarding—why are some people so committed to vandalism and destruction?

When foods, goods, and all the gifts of nature are so bountiful—why are some of us not even able to have one loaf of bread?

When nature is so sparkling with beauty—why do we keep spoiling and polluting it?

When each life is so precious, so sacred and so divine—why do some people insist on profaning and desecrating it?

Why, dear Lord, why?

Please, Lord, put the right answers in our minds and hearts and words and deeds, Your answers, Lord.

Shame on Me

Dear Lord,

For some time, I thought that I had nothing to do with Your crucifixion.

I wasn't there.

Pontius Pilate did it. The Roman soldiers did it. The Jewish people did it.

The hell with them all. I had nothing to do with it.

Until today, dear Lord, this was what I thought.

Today there are wars going on in East Europe, in the Middle East, in Africa. Today there is violence, and more violence, in our streets. People are killing people.

I did not do anything to stop it. I simply watched.

This is also what happened 2000 years ago, when we crucified You.

Shame on me.

Today, I realized that I was there in that crowd shouting for Your crucifixion. I carefully managed to let You bear Your cross. Then I stood in the crowd, from a well-measured distance to watch You die.

Shame on me.

Please, Lord, forgive me for I did not know what I was doing.

One-Minute Vacation

Dear Lord,

I am always so anxious and so eager to have things done right away. I hurry as if I was the only one who had to do them all, forgetting that You are still there.

I am always in a hurry, Lord, to have, to do, to think, to see the far away harvest at this moment, right now.

I am always in a hurry! Working, eating, walking, sitting down, and standing up. There is the feeling that I must do it before anyone else does.

Slow me down, dear Lord, slow me down.

Lord, give me, amidst the darkness of the night and the competitions of the day, the stillness of the everlasting hills.

Lord, give me, amidst the tensions of my desires and the pressures of my job, the smoothness of singing streams.

Lord, give me, amidst all these speedy machines, the calmness of the remote desert.

Lord, give me, amidst these instant artificial buildings, the solidity of the rocky mountains, and, amidst the everlasting traditions, give me to savor the enduring varieties of the changing seasons.

Lord, help me to have a good night sleep.

Lord, teach me the art of taking a one-minute vacation once in a while.

Lord, Teach me today to look at a flower and enjoy pure pleasure in the flower.

Lord, convince me to chat with a friend today, to make a new friend today, smile at a child playing and read an enjoyable poem today.

Lord, make me happy, like the cardinal that likes so much the tree by my window.

Who am I, after all, dear Lord?

Can I trace the pattern of a single bee?

Can I understand the miracle of a birth?

Can I fashion one single bird?

Can I let the sun rise before its time or cause a sunset before its schedule?

Who am I, Lord, who am I?

Slow me down, dear Lord, slow me down.

Let me taste my food today instead of just swallowing it.

Let me observe the sun and the moon today, how they rise and how they set.

Let me play with a child today and also with my dog and learn from them that the little child in me is still alive and well.

Let me be "unproductive" today and understand that there is in life something more productive than just producing merchandises.

Let me listen to the song of a bird today, for its message is Yours.

Let me watch the night sky and the stars today, for they speak to me of You.

Let others be in the forefront today, for I will have others opportunities and for You know what You are doing with me.

Let me read a good book today and listen to "The Four Seasons" and "The Messiah" and "The Ninth Symphony" and love them again.

Let me pet my pet today, for petting is the gift of now.

Let me wonder today, for wonder is just wonders-full.

Let me turn off my TV today and by doing so turn down all these unnecessary so-called attractions—and why should a noise be constantly in my house anyway?

Let me learn to let go, Lord, even if I know how hard letting go is. But I also know how better off I will be.

Let me walk today, just walk, not to get somewhere. And let me see things as if I see them for the first time.

Let me be aware of all that surrounds me at this moment and of You, the One who is behind them all. How wonderful they are!

Let me keep life simple. Let me take care of today.

Tomorrow, I know, will take care of itself.

Let me count Your many, many blessings, Lord, slowly, slowly, one by one, with a grateful heart.

And thank You, Lord, for I am never alone.

For Ever

Dear Lord,

    You have given me so many things.

    One more thing I now want to beg of You. Grant me the ability to keep thanking You for ever and ever. Amen.

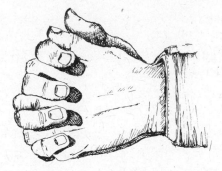

Small Acts of Love

Lord,

Help me to think well of others and also to speak well of them. For the tongue can be violent too. Sharper than a sword can a tongue be. I know it, dear Lord, I know it. Should I remind You what kind of people You put with me all the way in my life? A tongue can leave scars and bitterness in the heart, only Your grace of forgiveness can heal.

Lord,

Take my tongue today, and inscribe upon it words of love to whom ever needs them.

Take my hands and help the one who is struggling to overcome a difficult time.

Take my feet and visit a sick, an aged, a frustrated or a lonely friend.

Take my voice and sing a beautiful song to someone who longs to celebrate life today in song.

Take my face and spread a good smile through it, for no one really knows how much good an innocent smile can do. Help me to smile three times today at that person who bothers me so much, and let me do it Your way, just to radiate Your peace and Your love.

Take my heart and pour Your love on everyone I meet today, regardless who they are.

Let me realize that every time I smile, every time I offer a hand, every time I give attention to someone, every time I say a good word, every time I provide a little hope to someone, every time I help in liberating someone from the burden of isolation, physical, moral or spiritual poverty, or just from the weight of the day, it is Christmas again.

Let me take time to really look at someone today, to really talk with someone, to really listen to someone, to enjoy a joke with someone, for our life has become in such a rush that we lost the sweetness of someone presence, and we grew hungry for love, the basic real food for survival.

Let me be happier and better today by making everyone I meet happier and better.

And let me constantly experience Your Divinity and Infinity in the smallest act of love. Amen.

Dirt

Lord

My feet are dirty.

Come over here, right now.

Put on that apron and pour water in Your bowl and wash my feet.

I know I am bold for asking such a thing, but I know also that I have no chance to be with You with all this dirt.

So, Lord, wash my feet, my head, my mind, my heart, my attitude, my deeds and my soul.

Don't leave anything out.

Let my heart be pure in You. Amen.

What Use Is There?

Dear Lord,

When people are hurting, what use is there in trying to find who is right and who is wrong?

When everyone is losing, what use is there in trying to score points over a father, a son, a mother, a daughter, a husband, a wife, a friend, even an enemy?

When everyone can benefit, what use is there in trying to destroy those who do not believe what we believe or those who are under a different sky, with a different skin color or different background or different way of life?

Aren't these, Lord, simple and obvious truths?

Lord, help me to believe and live these simple and obvious truths, and extend my love to everyone, everywhere. Amen.

Delight

Lord,

I still dare to delight in things, even if I wanted to delight only in You.

Grant me that courage to be rooted, always in You first.

Then I would learn the way to delight in many things.

When I am with You, dear Lord, I will be sure that things will happen Your way.

Then my delight will be holy, and I will be complete.

Help Me to Help You

Lord,

Teach me how to be available today to anyone who needs me. Teach me how to be present, to all whom I meet today.

We have discovered medicines for almost all kind of diseases, but for the suffering of loneliness, or of feeling unwanted or having no one, we couldn't create a pill. Only a loving presence can heal this kind of suffering.

Lord, aren't You that lonely person, the frustrated one, the unwanted one I meet everyday?

Lord, aren't You also the only one who can help me to bring some comfort, support, or loving ears and tongue and hands and heart to that abandoned one?

Lord, I know You are with us forever in the needy, the sick, the prisoner, the hungry, and I certainly know that You are the One who takes care of the needy, the sick, the prisoner and the hungry.

Please Lord, help me to help you.

The Cross

Dear Lord,

You asked us one time to take up our cross and follow You.

Ok, dear Lord, ok! I am following You.

But why You don't give me a cross I can carry? Why do I have always the biggest one, the wrong one for me?

Wouldn't You make it, for once, the right cross for me?

Sometimes, when I face up to reality—my destiny, I tremble. I have the feeling of not having started my life yet. Plus, there are too many problems, dear Lord, with my family, with my work, in my past, in my present, and certainly in my future. Too many crosses and problems are mine.

Why should I carry all this? Why?

At one point, I even came to the conclusion to doubt You.

I doubted whether or not You were there. I was depressed, frustrated, skeptical, and revolted. I cursed heavens and earth and the day of my birth too, as Job did in the past.

But when I came to realize how You carried Your cross and how You faced reality and how You revolted against the hypocrisy of the status quo of Your time and You were not afraid of the torture of Your execution, I calmed down. I again followed You in the way of the cross.

The way of the cross is suffering indeed. But it also is the understanding for the mission You came to accomplish and Your faithfulness and obedience to it until the end.

Strange how we turned things upside down! That cross You were hung up on, is made pretty now. A piece of jewelry. A fashion. An important source of income. While your cross was ugly, dirty, full of blood and smelling death. With your collapse upon it, collapsed also all our phony successes and all our vain criteria and standards. How absurd and silly they were!

We celebrate Your birth, but ignore Your life.

We try not to miss the solemnities of Your death and resurrection, but we miss the opportunity to let them change us each day.

We are called after Your name, but we don't follow what Your name taught us.

You failed, it seemed; we want to succeed.

No, You did not play the Big Shot, the Superman, the Great Guy, the Mighty King who came down from the cross and had his armies fight for Him.

You just surrendered Your soul to the Father, for us.

You died.

It seemed, You failed.

When I think about your cross, my cross, even if it is bigger than I can carry, seems next to Yours insignificant.

Lord, help me to carry my cross the way You did, and understand my calling and be faithful to it. The way of the cross is also understanding and faithfulness.

Please, Lord, allow me to understand. And if I cannot understand, please Lord, keep my faith strong enough until I can understand. Amen.

Take

Dear Lord,

Take my liberty, for I cannot give it to you.

Take my memory, for I am fearful to be too attached to it.

Take my understanding, for the simple idea of losing it, cripples me.

Take my heart, for it scares me.

Take whatever I have that You have given me, Lord: keep it, for I do not want it back.

In spite of myself, Lord, save me.

When I am with You, I am satiated. With You, I feel healthy, wealthy, wise and whole.

Beside You, Lord, I need nothing. Amen.

Relationships

Dear Lord,

I never understood why I was attracted to certain people more than others, and to this particular person in a very special way.

Please take this attraction, also my thoughts and feelings and everything in me, and use them all for Your purposes.

Let my relationships with others, and especially with this special one, unfold according to Your will.

Aren't true relationships special assignments of Your Spirit?

Let your Spirit blueprint the path of awareness, growth and understanding with each person I am dealing with.

Let the combination of our energies do the most to further Your plan of salvation.

Dear Lord,

Let my relationships be holy. Amen.

Give Me

Lord,

    Give me strong health
      to do my work.

    Give me my work
      to keep my health strong.

    Give me health and work both
      to brighten my life.

    Give me life
      till my work is done,
      and my health is gone.

Lord,

    Give me life fully!
      While I am alive,
      and to be full of life,
      as long as I live,
      for a full life is possible,
      only if it is haunted by You,
      anywhere, anytime.

Lord,

    You alone are
    my health, my wealth and my life.

Scales

Dear Lord,

I carry scales so dearly in my mind, take them all away.

Take away all my prejudices, all my judgmental attitudes and all my secret attachments to racism, ethnicity, chauvinism, and all other aspects of segregation and discrimination.

Open my eyes, mind and heart, Lord, to see my brothers and sisters' beauty, because each one is Your child. Amen.

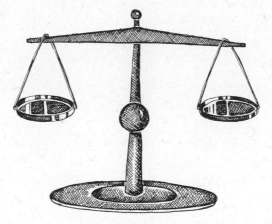

I Haven't Trusted You

Dear Lord,

For some time, as You remember, I haven't trusted You.

I used to surrender my thoughts, dreams, travels, pleasures, plans and even my career. But I never thought to surrender my romantic relationship, and especially not my way of thinking.

What I thought it was the most important to me I thought I better handle it myself.

I thought You didn't know how to handle it Yourself! I was afraid to leave it in Your hands, God knows what You would do with it. You may turn it upside down. I didn't trust You.

I never realized that what was the most important to me, was the most important to surrender to You.

To place something in Your hands, dear Lord, is the real guarantee for its protection.

To keep it myself means to snatch from You and grab and clutch and possess and manipulate and control it and leave You out.

How silly I was!

Lord, I trust You.

I don't pray to fall in love and to have a job and to do things my way.

I want the experience of love. I want bread on the table.

I want to know the way.

I leave the results of this situation in Your hands.

I know You are the way.

Help me to surrender my ways.

I want to trust You all the way.

May Your will for me be done. Amen.

Wonderful

Dear Lord,

Let me be with wonderful people today.
Not only that, Lord,
But let me be wonderful myself, too.

Above all, let me realize how wonderful I am by
realizing that I am the son of God.

There is nothing to compare with being the son of God.
There is nothing. Amen.

Just In Case

Dear Lord,

Like that foolish rich in Your Gospel (Luke 12:16-21), I built my own barns.

Just in case.

I secured myself with the barn of all kinds of insurances — life insurance, home insurance, car insurance, health insurance, dental insurance. . .

Lord, it was just in case.

Otherwise who can afford to pay the bills? Isn't insurance a human wisdom, dear Lord?

I did it, just in case.

I built the barn of savings in an insured bank.

Just in case.

I built the barn of possessions and more possessions, even if, instead of consuming them, they consumed me.

It was only, just in case.

I built the barn of knowing the right people, in the right places, for the right time, for the reasons of the world.

Just in case.

I built the barn of housing, the looks, fame, power, success and manipulation.

Just in case.

I built also, in a more subtle way, the barn of the vast collection of fine things, for the golden years in which I can relax and enjoy them.

And I carefully built the tomorrow barn, the biggest of all, for the rainy days, the "who knows what is going to happen" and the eventual disaster ahead.

Just in case.

And somehow I never thought about the other tomorrow, the day when things will no longer help me and when I stand before You to tell You how safe were the barns I built.

Dear Lord,

I fear what I guess You are going to ask me—if I fed the hungry, visited the prisoner, took care of the sick.

Dear Lord,

Free me from all these fears that make me build barn after barn after barn.

Let me, Lord, place this day, this only moment that exists, into Your hands.

You are my sole real security, for I rely upon Your promise: "I am with you."

You are indeed.

You proved it, as I remember, when you fed the thousands of people who followed You out of town.

Those who came to listen to Your word, THE WORD, received enough bread and fish to eat. They were not worried about food.

Lord, I am not going to worry either.

Lord, I want to trust You.

Please Lord,

Strengthen my trust and deepen my understanding.

I love You.

Amen.

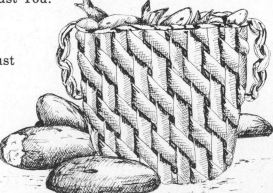

Use Me

Dear Lord,

Use me to radiate love, peace, joy—Your Presence.

Use my hands, my feet, my eyes, and my tongue to demonstrate Your message and spread Your presence into here and now.

Use my heart, my mind and the talents and abilities You've granted me, to serve others by spreading Your love.

Use my job as one means that will contribute to building a more beautiful earth, and hasten the coming of Your Kingdom on earth.

Use my smile to spread joy and more joy.

Let me play skillfully my part in Your plan of salvation for all, Lord.

Dear Lord,

Please Use me as an instrument of Your will.

Use me to radiate You.

Fear

Dear Lord,

Sometimes things scare me. Not that they are scary, but I am just terrified.

Even though I do have what it takes for not being afraid — nice family, good friends, health, credentials, talents, education, looks, job, house, money—I still feel very often paralyzed.

This fear is not coming from outside, really. It is not from the government. It is not from someone who needs to control me. It is not from someone who carries a weapon. It is not from any possible calamity. I am just afraid.

I am afraid of being with others, and afraid of being alone.

I am afraid of being like anyone else, and afraid of being different from anyone else.

I am afraid of being too silly, and afraid of being too serious.

I am afraid of being a sinner, and afraid of being a saint.

I am afraid this isn't the right job for me, and afraid it is.

I am afraid of being a failure, and afraid of being a success.

I am afraid people won't like me, and afraid they do.

I am afraid this isn't the right relationship, and afraid it is.

I am afraid of death, and afraid of life.

I am afraid of my past, afraid of my present, and afraid of my future.

I am often just afraid.

That is why I escaped.

Maybe this degree will reassure and strengthen me, or maybe this job, this book, this game, this mask, this seminar, this therapist, this author, this relationship, this diet, this pill, this drug, this addiction, this cigarette, this dish, this champagne, this insurance, this safety lock, this project, or even this act of charity or this retreat.

No cure.

Nothing worked.

I remained afraid until the day I read what You said: "It is I. Do not be afraid" (Matthew 14:27).

Then, I concentrated on You.

Then, I changed my perception.

Then, I realized that miracles happen by just changing perceptions.

Then, I was no longer afraid.

"Lord, tell me to come to You across the water."

Lord, "Save me" (Matthew 14:28-30).

Bridges

Lord,

Help us to build bridges between two shores, two persons and two nations.

Teach us to understand other people, to listen to them and appreciate what they stand for.

Teach us what responsibility towards others and ourselves really means.

Teach us what to speak, clearly, honestly and lovingly.

Teach us the difference between patriotism, nationalism, fidelity, loyalty, attachment, detachment, solidity and growth.

Teach us to support all the international and global organizations that bring people together and enjoy the same sense of human concern.

God knows how much we tried, how much we've failed!

Please, Lord, give us a hand.

Until We Are Two No More

Dear Lord,

    Think through my mind,
        until Your ideas are my ideas too.

    Love through my heart,
        until Your feelings are my feelings too.

    Make decisions through my will,
        until Your will is my will too.

    Speak through my lips,
        until Your words are my words too.

    Give to me grace. Take from me doubt. Prune me.
        Transform me—You alone know what is good for me.

    Be with me, around me, on the left of me, on the right
        of me, behind me, before me, above me, beneath me,
        within me,

    Until we are two no more. Amen.

Newspaper and Meditation

Dear Lord,

I love to read the newspaper. If I do not have time in the morning, I try not to miss it, before I go to bed.

I want to know what is happening in Your world.

I must know this, Lord.

I am supposed to be up to date on world and national affairs, and I like to give some opinions on all of that too.

But, one day, dear Lord, I realized while discussing things with a friend, that there was no big difference between me, the Christian who cares about religion, and my friend who is completely indifferent toward any religion.

There must be something wrong here, somewhere, dear Lord. In the way we understand religion, in me, or somewhere else? No one who lives his faith can have the outlook of someone who does not have faith. History is not human only; You are, dear Lord, very much involved in it. There are not two histories for humankind. There is only one.

So, dear Lord, wouldn't You help me to overcome my superficiality by granting me the faculty to be able to read between and especially above the lines of my newspaper, beyond persons and beyond history, according to the outlook of your Gospel. Help me to detect the real values for building the Kingdom through the vehicle of human events, struggle for greater freedom, justice, responsibility and dignity for individuals and nations, education, art, effort towards peace, unity and settlement of conflicts. And, dear Lord, let me do something, if these things come to be lacking. Let me try to do at least a little part of what you may have done if you were to read the newspaper yourself.

Dear Lord, let me decipher, when I read the newspaper, the routes that lead to the Kingdom, and let me commit myself to work for a little more compassion in this troubled world.

Let the newspaper be today not a satisfaction for my curiosity, but a vehicle for my meditation and for more love.

Amen.

Meaning

Dear Lord,

Tonight, I heard the anguish and the deep sighing of men and women all over the earth.

A bitterness was surfacing with their cries. An inner rebellion was taking place.

They had lost the meaning in their walk of life.

Some of them took God out of their lives, to keep Him safe." Some others just refused Him. And some others did not know that He was there. All of them did not see that He was the meaning of their lives, as a sap in a tree, or leaven in a bread, or life in a body.

Tonight, I am not going to "defend the rights of God," as an activist who is busy to post up his symbols on a wall, or have his name in a rule or a law or over a jacket.

Tonight, I am not going to try to be an "apostolic," zealot of a missionary.

Tonight, I am going to ask You in a special way, dear Lord, to be more visible in my own life.

Tonight, I want You to be more within myself, so when I am among them, they will see You through my heart, my mind, my living flesh, and my human actions. Isn't this, after all, what the meaning of the union and communion between the Creator and the creature is all about?

Tonight, I must go back to the Center-God-Love and let this love embody my every deed.

Tonight, I am going to walk in Your steps with Your feet, as Simon, the Cyrenean did one time, when he helped to carry Your cross and when he forgot about the cross and kept his sight only on You and on Your steps. You were central in his vision.

Then, Lord, perhaps if all these men and women see me walking among them as someone who keeps adjusting his steps to Your steps, they will rediscover their meaning, and their anguish will be no more. For they can walk with us too.

Confused

Dear Lord, aren't You confused by now?

How many people, dear Lord, are asking for so many contradictory things?

These people need rain. Those people need sunshine.

These ask for money, and more money. Those think the less money they have, the closer to You they become.

These ask for a special favor to be able to follow the rules. Those ask for the same favor to be able to change the rules.

These pray for victory over those, and those pray for victory over these. And all of them are supposedly allies around You. And You are in the middle. What are You going to do? Aren't You confused?

Even myself, dear Lord, how many times I asked you contradictory things? How many times I asked things which were just the contrary of what I really needed?

Dear Lord, we are confusing beings, indeed.

Help us discern truth from our confusion.

Help us, Lord, to ask for what we really need, You!

Run With Me

Dear Lord,

It is morning again.
The alarm o'clock rang at five.
I have to get up,
      off to the bathroom,
      I'll wash up,
      dress,
      have a cup of coffee, and grab something to eat,
      and then run.

Yet today, I do not feel in the mood to do all that.

I'd rather go back to bed, pull up over my head, all the covers and pillows I have, forget everything, and sleep.

I feel tired, tired, tired, and I have to run again.

Dear Lord, what am I running for after all? Why am I running?

Is it because everybody runs in the morning?
Is it because this is how to make money?
Is it because this is how mornings are supposed to begin?
Is it because God wants it this way?
These things are difficult for me to understand.
I am not even interested in knowing the real reasons for running.

What I am interested in is to know that You know where and why I am running and that You are running with me and You will lead the way. Lord, You ARE the way.

Knowing this will really help me.

Let's run! Amen.

In the Traffic

Dear Lord,

Enough is enough. I want to get home.

Here it is, Friday. I worked all day all week long. Here I am stuck in this traffic.

I am so tired of working, waiting, sweating and listening to this stupid radio.

Lord, I want to get home.

I wish I could fly over all these cars and just get home. I want to take a shower, put my shorts on and relax under my tree in the backyard.

These people around me here are so annoying! I am supposed to be patient, gentle and really human.

Look at this old lady; she hardly can see where she is going. Look at this young fellow; he is smoking his cigarette, and listening to his very loud music as he was alone on this road. Look at this young lady and look at this man and look at this car and that car and all those people who are trying to cross the street. What a chaos!

It is too much, dear Lord. I hope you are not going to ask me to be just patient.

I cannot do it alone. Please Lord, do this with me. Stay with me.

Thank you, Lord, for sweating with me, for being tired with me and for being patient with me.

Alone, I couldn't have done it. There is no way. Stay, Lord, stay with me. Amen.

Good Night

Dear Lord,

Allow me to sleep well tonight.

All these fears I had today, let them evaporate and dissipate one by one.

Free me from my anxieties.

Free me from my false worries and concerns.

Take water and wash the wounds I have caused to my neigbhors.

Take fire and burn away my lies, masks and fluctuating attitudes.

Take light and flash through my past, and enlighten my present and brighten my future.

Take surrender and plant it in my greed and especially my greed for time—I am still greedy for time to be success-ful, time to perform, excel, produce, time to be effective and useful, time to make money, time to do what I want to do.

Lord, dry the tears I have provoked in the eyes of those who still like me.

Lord, forgive my sins and mistakes and omissions.

Lord, infect my stinginess and poor calculations with Your generosity.

Lord, help me to carry my heavy baggage of whatever kind—physical, mental, emotional, cultural—and projects and plans and dreams.

Lord, free me from my anxieties and false worries and concerns, and grant me Your peace, so that I may wake up refreshed tomorrow.

Good night, Lord.

Purpose

Dear Lord,
    Give my life a sense of purpose.

Lord,
    We both know You are that purpose.

Lord,
    Be that purpose. Amen.

Zorba

Dear Lord,

The figure of Zorba puzzles me.
He lives life to the full.
He loves this earth; he smells it, tastes it, and finds
all of it good.
He is not a "saint"; he is human.
He makes mistakes.
He does good things.
He laughs.
He cries.
He meets others. He interacts with them, he meets his
needs and he meets their needs.
He gets involved with life. He lives life.
He is human.
Sacred is life for him; something to be celebrated! Life
is something holy.
Nothing of Yours for him is profane.

Dear Lord,

This is what You did too.
You never classified things.
You never divided things as "holy" and "profane."
You liked to eat, to drink, to be merry with friends.
You laughed.
You cried.
You were not neutral, passive, and You didn't surround
Yourself by neutral, passive people either.

All the people You chose were not well-balanced, lukewarm,
apathetic and passionless.
Peter was impulsive, active, energetic, exuberant. Paul
was vibrant, intense, sharp, committed, able to experience
ecstasy as well as depression. John was sensitive, tender
and loving.
You loved life as it is, and You did everything according
to Your Father's will.

Lord,

Teach me to celebrate life as You did and as Zorba does.

I want to be joyous and free as You were, as Zorba is and each true son of God is.

I don't want to act "saintly"—this is something terribly boring. I want to be really human — really divine.

The more human I am, the more saint I want to become. I want to be real.

And I know, when the game of rhetoric and philosophical, theological and political speculations ends, I know that You are here, in a cradle, on a cross, across the road, across the table, in the church, in the marketplace, in every aspect of our life, and I must love You right here, right now in myself, in my neighbor and everywhere.

So, come Lord, enter into my heart—deep within my emotions, feelings and passions, my whole spirit—and reveal Your presence even in the core of my being.

As long as You are not the life of my life, I will cling to people and things to find the warmth of some kind of belonging in those places.

If You are there, I will feel free and then I will let go all false forms of foreign belongings.

Lord,

Give me the courage to live fully and spontaneously, even though it may lead to unintentional mistakes, and to take discerned risks, even though they may lead to pain.

But let me always be on Your side, even if I commit errors.

Give me a heart of real flesh and blood, a heart that feels and loves and adores You, and delights in others, because of You.

And Lord,

Take my joys and sorrows,
Take my hopes and disappointments,
Take my successes and failures,
Take my privileges and calamities,
Take my virtues and sins,
Take my peace and violence,
Take my gladness and sadness,
Take my pleasures and wounds,
Take my nights and days,
Take my ups and downs,
Take all my impulses, and longings, and frustrations, as well as all my delights, and fun, and ecstasies, and use them to make a perfect rainbow arch in Your heavens.

Take me as I am and make Your dream, my dream: to become a saint by becoming more human in this life You transformed into sacrament.

Lord, help me to live to the fullest by being more human and saint.

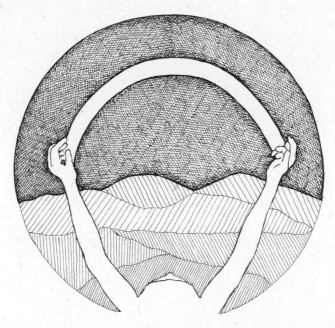

Be Me

Lord,

You are terrible!

It is hard to live with You.

It is impossible to live without You.

I love You. I love You. I love You. Do You hear me? Do You understand what I am saying?

Please make of this wild and bold journey of faith, a path to You, then, to the real me.

Please stay with me on this path. I cannot walk it alone.

Be in me. Breathe in me. See in me. Hear in me. Taste in me. Touch in me. Feel in me. Think in me. Be the life of my life. Be me.

What I do does not really count much, when it comes to what I am.

Lord, be me.

I want to be You.

Long journey! Hard work!

With the Holy Spirit, we can do it.

Be me.

I want to be real. I mean, I want to be You.

Let the Holy Spirit take care of the whole thing. Amen.

About the Author

IF YOU WANT TO IDENTIFY JEAN MAALOUF DO NOT ASK HIM, "When is your birthday?," or "What do you do for a living?," or "Where do you live?," or "What are the color of your eyes?" Ask him rather, "What do you live for?," or "What keeps you going?," or "Where do you stand from this or that?," or "How do you perceive things?" Then, he will tell you, how he does the most ordinary things but in an extraordinary way. Then, he will explain how he keeps his intuitive heart and questioning mind wide open to detecting what life stores for him, either through schooling (he holds a *doctorat en philosophie/sciences des religions* from Sorbonne University, Paris, France), or by traveling, reading, playing, or just living and doing what he happens to be doing at the moment. And he will tell you also how much he likes words, sounds, colors, silence, laughter, wonder, and especially meditation and prayer. The Divine Presence, by being the context of his daily routine, makes his ordinary actions so magical, that all his life has become a quest for the freedom to be open to interact with what is, and respond to the smallest emotional overtones and nuances of life and living. And by taking the risk of experiencing the Divine Presence in this way, he insists to celebrate his God, who has become the very Reality of his daily life. No wonder there are many facets for his personality. Indeed, in his life, he has been a hard working employee, a baker, a salesman, a library cataloguer, a translator, a journalist, an educator, a professor, a poet, a philosopher, a humanist, a researcher, an ecumenist, a counselor, a lecturer, a peacemaker, a writer, a lover of everything and everyone—his way or worshiping, being alive and genuine.

Besides the numerous inspirational and educational articles he has written, he is the author of *Le Mystère du Mal dans l'Oeuvre de Tielhard de Chardin* (Cerf, 1986), *Touch a Single Leaf* (Mulberry Books, 1993), and contributor to *Le Réenchantement du Monde* (Publisud, 1993). He is an independent, free and uncompromising thinker. His integrity compels him to say what he wants to say, even if it is not the thing one would expect or like to hear. He lives in Connecticut, but he is very often in New York City and Paris. He feels at home everywhere he happens to be, because he feels at home with himself in the first place. And this is only a part of what he lives for. He lives to radiate that sense of integration and warmth, love and peace that should characterize the one human family in this one single world. He also thinks that a contemplative attitude is the most transforming element, and that it opens us to the true realization of ourselves, or others, and of everything in the creation. With all this perception, he has never lost from his heart the innocence of the magical child within, neither has he lost sight of the message—the essential connection—he carries in the depth of his soul; two things that keep him going with wonder, awe and dreams for global growth.

Thus the creation of *Bold Prayers from the Heart*.

This book, which unfolds a deeper awareness of our communion with God and His creation, is a direct human experience of the Divine Presence. This is not, by any means, an abstract book on spirituality. It is an existential book that shows rather how practically we connect with the Divine Being by whom we exist and do our things. The other connections that we certainly need to use to improve our lives, important as they are, remain very secondary when compared to this most essential one, the connection to God. This book is a living chapter from what can be called "incarnational spirituality" or "integration spirituality" or "existential spirituality," in which spirituality is not an escape from the world, and sanctity does not conflict with being fully human. Jesus Christ was fully divine and fully human, wasn't He? The whole of our daily living is supposed to be a spiritual path, a "walking theology," a prayer, a human experience of God. Our humanity—all that we are—is the clue to God's truth. Looking for a higher truth than in life itself, is a useless effort. God is not elsewhere. God is LIFE. This is why some of us have such a passion and zeal for True Life. The miracle of the ordinary is this extraordinary realization which transforms our daily actions through and into prayer.

Is this a new ascetic practice? It is not new. Is sanctity an "ecclesiastical item" that belongs only or mainly to a person of the hierarchy? Certainly not. Is this a shift in our perception? It certainly is, or at least a major focus adjustment in our approach to the spiritual life. The truth is that our daily actions become one continuous prayer, when we grasp the secrets of cleansing the doors of our perception and of adjusting our focus. All other connections remain unsettled and elusive, unless the essential one is on focus.

This book was lived during a certain number of years. This book was prayed. Then this book was written. That is why it so genuine, so striking, so alive, and sometimes so very provocative, even though it is written with an astonishing simplicity. Maybe, because it is written this way, it sparkles spontaneously and clearly the faith in action. Indeed everything is possible, the seemingly impossible thing and the most ecstatic joy included, when they are asked for on one's knees, in prayer.

Such a book, then, with its powerful radiance of the human-divine integration and its compelling appeal for the magical alchemy of our daily living of it, is a milestone in the transmutation of each of us, and a leading beacon in a critical moment of individual and world transformation.